How to Use Reference Materials

How to Use Reference Materials

BY BERNICE MACDONALD

A Language Skills Concise Guide
FRANKLIN WATTS
New York | London | Toronto | Sydney | 1980

Library of Congress Cataloging in Publication Data

MacDonald, Bernice.
How to use reference materials.

(A Language skills concise guide)
Includes index.
SUMMARY: Introduces the Dewey Decimal and the
Library of Congress classification systems, card
and book catalogs, and reference sources. Also
discusses using and evaluating materials and taking notes.
1. Reference books—Juvenile literature. 2. Libraries and students—Juvenile literature. [1. Reference books. 2. Libraries] I. Title. II. Series:
Language skills concise guide.
Z711.M2   011'.02   80–14525
           ISBN 0–531–04134–4

Contents

How to Use Reference Materials

My thanks to Henry Gilfond
for his assistance in
preparing this book.

Introduction

For one reason or another, we are always looking for some piece of information—an address, a telephone number, how to get to the ball park, a museum, a party. And there is usually a handy reference book around to help us find the information we want—an address book, a telephone book, a card index, a street map. Sometimes we look for the meaning of a word in our dictionary. If we want to know the shortest route from one town to another, we can consult a road map, perhaps kept in the glove compartment of the family car. And there is undoubtedly a cookbook in the kitchen that will give us the directions for making a roast, a stew, or a dessert.

There are times, however, when the information we need cannot be found in our homes. Maybe we need to write a report on some historical event, on some ecological problem, or on some new development in the world of science. Perhaps we need to have some details about the life of a notable person, about a particular period in our history, or about the events leading to some scientific discovery. To get this information, we generally need to go to the library, to dig into the many and varied reference books, periodicals, and pamphlets the library has on its shelves.

Libraries have a large number of encyclopedias, indexes, atlases, dictionaries, bibliographies, and almanacs. They have current and back issues of magazines and newspapers. Many have microfilm to provide the researcher with written material otherwise too bulky to store. And increasingly, libraries have computerized information banks that, at the touch of a button, will give us much if not all of the data we need.

The library is a virtual storehouse of information, but to get the particular information we are looking for, we need to know where in the library that information is stored. We have to know how to select and locate particular books, magazines, and pamphlets. For that, we need to know how libraries are organized. We need to be able to read library card indexes and understand how library books are arranged on the different shelves. In other words, to get the information we seek most quickly and efficiently, we need to develop *library skills.*

This book will introduce you to the library and to the librarian. It will introduce you to the library's basic reference sources. It will help you to acquire the very necessary skills that are basic to the search for knowledge.

The importance of acquiring library skills cannot be overstated. Without them research of any kind is almost impossible. For verifying data, for doing reports and projects for school, or for gathering information for your business or professional life, these skills are essential. And the continued use of them will serve not only to improve your research abilities but will also make research a pleasurable as well as profitable exercise for you.

What will it take to develop these skills? As any

professional athlete will tell you, practice and more practice are what develop our skills in any of our endeavors. The better our research skills, the more quickly and effectively we can work, and the better the results of our labors.

Part One of this book will introduce you to the library and its basic resources. It will describe the skills you will need to develop if you are to use the library's resources effectively. And it will introduce you to the librarian. The librarian is a human reference source, always willing to aid and direct us in our search for information. There is no one who can help us more in acquiring library skills than the librarian. Alex Haley has said that in tracing the hundreds of years of history for his epic work *Roots,* librarians were the ones who helped him most. The librarian, he said, was his greatest ally during his twelve-year journey of painstaking research.

Part Two of this book describes general and specific reference sources that may be found in all but the smallest libraries. You will be introduced to encyclopedias, dictionaries, atlases, bibliographies, and special materials such as pamphlets and microfilm. School and public libraries have at least one of each kind of reference source described in this book. You will learn what kind of information can be found in each of these sources and how this information is arranged within each book. You will be told approximate lengths of articles in a certain number of these sources, the style in which these articles are written, the approximate number of illustrations, the physical format, and special features.

Part Three of this book approaches research from the perspective of doing a research report or researching a speech. You will find many tips in this section that will not only help you in assignments for school, but will further increase your general library skills and help you in evaluating research materials.

The student, the scholar, the professional researcher—all find the library a comfortable and interesting place, even an exciting place. They move from catalog to encyclopedia, from microfilm to newspaper. They might read of the day a man first walked on the moon or perhaps listen to a speech made by Martin Luther King, Jr. Their search is absorbing. It is much like seeking for buried treasure. We may not be able to buy groceries with what we find, but the unearthing of some hidden items of knowledge, stored among all the vast wealth of information our culture has collected, can prove to be a most rewarding and pleasurable experience.

Part One

The Classification of Library Resources

Libraries, in the simplest sense, are places where large quantities of printed material—books, pamphlets, and periodicals—are housed and organized. Of course many libraries contain other items as well, such as photographs, records, and tapes. But printed matter still forms the bulk of the material stored in the library, and librarians are specialists in the organization of such material. When we arrange our own books on our bookshelves at home, we may be considered to be doing a task a librarian would perform.

Some people arrange their books alphabetically, according to the names of the authors in their library. Some people arrange their books by color, size, or subject matter. Alistair Cooke, the noted British authority on American culture, arranges his books geographically, starting with books on California and moving east, north, and south. Some people don't arrange their books at all.

School and public libraries, with their huge collections of books and broad range of subject matter, have developed a very formal system of organization for their books. This system includes a formal classification, or listing, of all the books in the library.

There are two major classification systems used

in American libraries today. Because it is an especially good system for small libraries, the majority of libraries use the Dewey Decimal Classification system. Some libraries, however, particularly large research and university libraries, use the Library of Congress system, which was first developed in 1897 to organize the vast collection of our national library.

Since all libraries are organized in basically the same way, no more than a nodding acquaintance with each of these two methods of organization, along with an understanding of how to use the library's card (or book) catalog, is necessary to make you feel quite at home in your own local or school library. And remember, if you have any trouble at all locating the particular material you seek, you can always ask the librarian to help you—to use the card catalog or even just to point out the proper shelf of books to you.

Let us now take a look at these two systems of library classification.

THE DEWEY DECIMAL CLASSIFICATION SYSTEM

This system was devised by the great nineteenth-century American librarian, Melvil Dewey. The system, first published anonymously in 1876, has been revised frequently, translated into many languages, and is now in its eighteenth edition. However, Dewey's basic idea of dividing all areas of knowledge into ten major classes has survived. Here is how the division looks:

000–099   General works
100–199   Philosophy
200–299   Religion
300–399   Social sciences (human relations)

400–499 Linguistics
500–599 Pure sciences
         (observations of the environment)
600–699 Applied sciences
         (manipulation of the environment)
700–799 Arts and recreation
800–899 Literature
900–999 Geography, History,
         and related disciplines

Each class, or area of knowledge, is further divided into ten classes, and then again into ten more, making a total of one thousand. Additional subdivisions are made by adding a decimal point and numbers after the first three digits in the original ten classes. The following is an example of how one of these original classes is broken down in library cataloging:

800—Literature

    810—American literature
    811—American poetry
    812—American drama
    813—American fiction
    814—American essays
    815—American oratory
    816—American letters
    817—American satire and humor
    818—American miscellany
    819—Canadian-English literature
    820—English literature
    830—German and other Germanic literatures
    840—French and related literatures
    850—Italian and related literatures
    860—Spanish and Portuguese literatures

870—Latin and other Italic literatures
880—Greek and Hellenic literatures
890—Other literatures

These categories are further subdivided by the use of additional numbers, decimal points, and more numbers, so that we may find more speedily the exact type of literature we want. For example, we have already seen that the number 800 on a book indicates that it is concerned with literature. By adding the number 11 to 800, giving us the number 811, the library tells us that this book, marked 811, is a book of American poetry. A decimal point and the number .01 added to 811, making it 811.01, tells us that the book so numbered is a book on the philosophy and theory of American poetry.

Some other classifications in the 811 category are:

811.03—Dictionaries, encyclopedias,
      concordances of American poetry
811.07—Study and teaching of American poetry
811.08—Collections of American poetry

Obviously, this system of classifying the vast number of books in the library makes the job of the researcher easier.

The one type of book that is not classified by number in the Dewey Decimal system is fiction. If you want to find a novel by John Steinbeck or a book of Ernest Hemingway's short stories, look for it on the library shelves reserved for fiction. Fiction in the library is shelved alphabetically by the author's last name.

THE LIBRARY OF CONGRESS CLASSIFICATION SYSTEM

The Library of Congress system, like the Dewey system, uses numbers to classify books. However, it also uses the letters of the alphabet. One letter is used to designate each separate branch of human knowledge —philosophy, music, social science, law, and so on. A second letter is added to the first letter to indicate a subdivision. For example, if you want a book dealing with philosophy and religion, you look for it among books labeled with the letter "B." If you want a book on psychology (a subdivision of philosophy and religion), you'll find it among books labeled "BF." Numbers are then added, up to 9999, for further subdivisions.

The Library of Congress needed this more detailed system to classify its library collection because of the enormous number of books, papers, pamphlets, periodicals, and other reading matter it amassed over the years. It might be noted that the Library of Congress has yet to use the letters I, O, W, X, and Y. These letters are being reserved for the future and expected growth of human knowledge.

Here is a brief summary of how the Library of Congress, with its vast wealth of material, subdivides its collection. A few further subdivisions of one letter are included.

A—General works
B—Philosophy and Religion
    BB—Philosophy (general)
    BF—Psychology
    BL—Religions, Mythology, Rationalism
    BM—Judaism
    BP—Islam, Bahaism, Theosophy

C—History and Auxiliary sciences
D—History and Topography excluding America
E–F—American History
G—Geography and Anthropology
H—Social sciences
J—Political sciences
K—Law
L—Education
M—Music
N—Fine arts
Q—Science
R—Medicine
S—Agriculture
T—Technology
U—Military science
V—Naval science
Z—Bibliography and Library science

The library arranges its books according to their classification numbers, more commonly referred to as call numbers. You will find books numbered 818 shelved right next to the books marked 817, and so on.

There is no need to memorize either classification system in order to determine the call number of a book you want. You need only to consult the library's card catalog. Once you know how to use the card catalog, finding a book will be a simple job.

The Card Catalog

The card catalog in a library lists every book in that library's collection. Small cards are kept in cabinets generally stationed near the front of the library, for easy access. These cabinets consist of a number of drawers, each alphabetically labeled—*A–Am, Am–Bo, Bo–Ci,* and so on. Each card in each drawer contains in one upperhand corner a call number, to tell us where in the library the book listed on that card may be found.

There are three main ways to find material in the card catalog. You can look up the title of a book, the name of an author, or the subject you are investigating. You can thumb through the *W* file, for example, if you want to know whether the book *Wolves in the City* is in the library. You would look through the *B* file to see if Gilda Berger's book, *The Gifted and Talented,* was part of the library's collection. Or, you could look through the cards in the drawer labeled *M–Mo* for a book on the history of Mexico.

One point to remember in looking up a book title: If the title starts with *A, An,* or *The,* the card will be filed alphabetically by the *second* word in its title. For example, the card for a book called *The New Oxford Dictionary* will be found among the *N* cards in the library.

In looking for authors' names, you look for the last name first. If two authors have the same last name, they are then listed alphabetically by first name.

There is more information on the catalog card than just call number, title, and author. There is also, usually, a date of publication, a publisher, a place of publication, the length of the book, the number of pages in the book, if and how the book is illustrated, and sometimes a short summary of the book.

We will see some examples of cards in a moment. But first, two others ways of finding materials in the card catalog should be mentioned. These are the *See* and *See also* cross-reference cards. As their name implies, these cards direct you to other parts of the card catalog. The *See* cards tell you your material will be found under *another* heading. The *See also* cards tell you that if you look under the headings suggested, you will find *additional* cards on the subject in other parts of the card catalog.

Let us now take a closer look at the way the cards in the card catalog make finding books in the library so simple.

Suppose someone has recommended to you a book on cooking by Craig Claiborne, the well-known gourmet, but you have forgotten the title. You thumb through the card catalog until you find the following card:

Claiborne, Craig   647.5951 C
    The Chinese Cookbook. Craig Claiborne
    & Virginia Lee. Photos by Bill Aller.
    Drawings by Barbra and Roderick Wells.
    Philadelphia, Lippincott, 1972. 451 p. ill.

The card not only tells you there is a coauthor of the book but also that the book includes photographs and by whom, drawings and by whom, the name of the publisher of the book, the date of the book's publication, and the number of pages in the book. The "ill." informs you that the book is illustrated.

On the other hand, if you recall only the title of this same book, you would look through the files for *The Chinese Cookbook* and find this card:

```
┌──────────────────────────────────────────────┐
│                                                │
│                                                │
│   The Chinese Cookbook          647.5951  C    │
│      Claiborne, Craig & Virginia Lee           │
│                                                │
│                                                │
└──────────────────────────────────────────────┘
```

Suppose, instead, you were interested in ancestor cults. You look up the subject in the card catalog and find the following:

```
┌──────────────────────────────────────────────┐
│                                                │
│                                                │
│                  Ancestor Cults               │
│                      See                       │
│                Ancestor Worship                │
│                                                │
│                                                │
└──────────────────────────────────────────────┘
```

This, of course, is a *See* card, referring you to another section of the card catalog. You would turn to that section to find a listing of books on the subject you want. This card simply means that books on ancestor cults will be found listed under ancestor worship.

The *See also* card carries more information. For example, if you were doing a project on world population, you might find the following card in the library catalog:

Population
See also subdivision. Population under name
of countries, cities, etc., and ethnic groups,
e.g. United States—population; Indians of
North America—population

It is obvious that this card, sending you to other sources, will help a great deal in the project at hand.

Looking for a book in the catalog, if you know the name of its author or the title of the book, is rather easy. Looking for books by their subject matter is a little more difficult. But if you learn to think of key words related to the subject matter, the job of getting to the material you want will be that much simpler.

For example, if you want information on the Five Civilized Tribes, you might look through the catalog for books listed under the heading "Indians of North America." If you want to do a paper on marathons, you are likely to find some useful books listed under the heading "Olympic Games."

Thinking in terms of headings and categories when you thumb through the library catalog will get you to your research material quickly.

Library Catalogs in Book Form

Some libraries, in addition to having cabinets of cataloged cards, have catalogs in the form of books. There is probably an author catalog, in which you can locate the books you need by checking the alphabetical listings for the authors of these books. There is probably also a title catalog for locating, in the same manner, books by their title. And there may also be a subject catalog, with subjects listed alphabetically. Under each subject in this catalog there will be a listing of authors and titles of books dealing with that subject.

This form of cataloging is becoming more and more popular with libraries and may well make the traditional card catalog obsolete.

Whichever you use, however, whether it be a catalog in book or card form, the alphabetical listing of books in a library's collection is essentially the same. It takes only a little time and practice to learn how to use it efficiently.

Part Two

Basic
Reference Sources

Most reference sources can be placed in one of two groups:

    (1). Those that contain the precise information that we are looking for. These include

          encyclopedias
          dictionaries
          atlases and gazetteers

    (2). Those that direct us to where we can find the precise information we want. These include

          indexes
          bibliographies
          directories

Both groups are designed for quick, frequent, and easy use, rather than browsing.

    You will usually find reference books in a separate section or room of the library. This section or room will be called, appropriately, the Reference Section or the Reference Room. You won't be able to take home books from this section. Reference books are meant to be used in the library only.

Here is a brief description of the various reference sources:

encyclopedias—overviews of subjects
dictionaries—information about words
atlases—maps and charts
indexes—location of specific information required
bibliographies—lists of books and other materials
directories—names and addresses of people or
    organizations
biographical dictionaries—information about people
almanacs—general facts and statistical information

ENCYCLOPEDIAS

The word *encyclopedia* comes from the ancient Greek words *enkyklios paideia,* meaning "entire circle of human knowledge." Aristotle, the ancient Greek philosopher, wrote the first encyclopedia. The oldest encyclopedia in the English language is the *Encyclopaedia Britannica,* first published in Scotland in the latter part of the eighteenth century. Of course no encyclopedia contains all there is to know on any given subject. And there are many reference books that contain the same information as the encyclopedia. But the encyclopedia is often a good place to start research on a broad topic or to get some background on an unfamiliar subject.

The three most widely used general encyclopedias today are

Encyclopedia Americana
Collier's Encyclopedia
Encyclopaedia Britannica

Each one is distinct in its arrangement, coverage, and emphasis of material. The best way to know which is most suitable for the work you are doing is to compare the three in terms of arrangement, length of articles, writing style, illustrations, physical format, and special features. Here is a description of each.

Encyclopedia Americana. New York: Americana Corporation, 1979. 30 volumes.

An excellent and dependable encyclopedia that emphasizes topics of American interest and modern scientific developments. Volume 30 contains an overall index.

Arrangement: Alphabetical by specific subject headings. 40,000 cross-references. Large index that is easy to use.

Length of Articles: Length varies from brief paragraphs to book-size articles. Average article length is 600 words, or half a page.

Writing Style: Clear and direct. The most technical subject matter is understandable to the average high school student.

Illustrations: 20,000 illustrations. Photographs, drawings, diagrams, charts, and graphs clarify the text.

Physical Format: Uncluttered appearance, with guide words at the top of the page.

Special Features: Approximately 40 percent of the articles are biographies. Full texts of important historical documents are included, such as the Emancipation Proclamation and the U.S. Constitution. Summaries of works of literature, art, and music are also included.

Encyclopaedia Britannica. Chicago: Encyclopaedia Britannica, 1980. 30 volumes.

Oldest and largest encyclopedia, noted for its emphasis on the humanities and literature and for its lengthy scholarly articles.

Arrangement: Essentially a reprint of the fifteenth edition (known as *Britannica 3*), which was published in 1974, this encyclopedia is divided into three parts: Propaedia (outline of knowledge), Micropaedia (ready reference and index), and Macropaedia (knowledge in depth). The one-volume Propaedia classifies knowledge into ten main categories, such as "the earth," "human life," and "art," and throughout the articles in this volume references are provided to articles in the Macropaedia. The ten-volume Micropaedia serves as a source of quick reference. It contains 102,000 brief articles that never exceed 750 words in length. The nineteen-volume Macropaedia is the main part of the encyclopedia, devoted to long and scholarly articles. Different color panels on the spine of each volume keep the three separate parts from being confused.

Length of Articles: In the ten-volume Micropaedia, articles are brief. In the nineteen-volume Macropaedia, they average 7,000 words on five double-column pages.

Writing Style: Most articles are written in a scholarly but readable style and are understandable to bright high school juniors and seniors.

Illustrations: Not heavily illustrated. Small diagrams, photographs, and maps are used, but color is limited.

Physical Format: Has a formal, dignified look, appropriate for a serious work of scholarship.

Special Features: Its most distinctive feature is its arrangement into the three parts described above. Other features include wide international coverage and boxes of statistical information for each country of the world.

Collier's Encyclopedia. New York: Macmillan Educational Corporation, 1979. 24 volumes.

Less scholarly than the *Americana* or *Britannica,* Collier's emphasizes modern subjects and is strong on sports. Volume 24 includes an index, a bibliography, and a study guide.

Arrangement: Alphabetical by broad subject headings. Because it is a broad-entry encyclopedia, the index in the final volume is essential.

Length of Articles: Articles range from a few lines to essays of seventy or more pages. Average length is one page.

Writing Style: Most popularly written of the three major encyclopedias.

Illustrations: 21,000 illustrations, excellent maps. Full-color illustrations accompany many articles.

Physical Format: Attractively designed, print is large and bold.

Special Features: Unlike other encyclopedias, *Collier's* places most of its references to further readings in the last volume, before the index. The titles for reference usually represent the best available works on the topic and are listed in graduated order, from simple to more difficult. There is also in the last volume a fifteen-page study guide to twenty-three subjects that directs students and teachers to appropriate articles in the encyclopedia.

DICTIONARIES

General dictionaries provide information such as spelling, pronunciation, derivation, and meaning about the words of a language. They are either *unabridged,* that is, complete, covering all the words of a language; or *abridged,* that is, a cut-down version of a larger dictionary. In learning how to use a dictionary as well as in selecting the kind of dictionary that will best suit your purpose, you should be alert to the following points:

How is pronunciation shown in the dictionary?
Is slang included?
Are definitions of words given in order of their historical or their current usage?
Does the dictionary contain quotations, maps, or pictures?
Does it list synonyms (words having similar meanings) or antonyms (words having opposite meanings) with its definitions of words?

The two unabridged dictionaries that are found in most libraries are:

Webster's Third New International Dictionary of the English Language. Springfield, Mass.: G. & C. Merriam Company, 1961.

This dictionary presents the language as currently used and includes words not usually regarded as proper English. It has 450,000 entries, many of which are scientific or technological words. Here is a sample entry in *Webster's Third New International:*

guard lock n 1: a tide lock at the mouth of a dock or basin or a lock for preventing flooding of a canal 2: a lock guarding the keyhole or bolt of another lock and having to be unlocked before the key of the main lock can be operated

Random House Dictionary of the English Language. New York: Random, 1966, 1979.

This is a relatively new dictionary that aims to catch up with our expanding vocabulary by including words currently in use in the English language. It has approximately 260,000 entries (updated about every two years) that include personal names, place names, and titles of literary works. Its definitions are more informal than *Webster's.* Here is an example:

drag bunt, Baseball, softball, a light bunt made by drawing the bat back as the ball is struck, causing it to roll on the ground.

INDEXES

The word *index* comes from the Latin *indicare,* meaning "to point out." As its name implies, an index indicates where information may be found; it does not give the actual information. *The Readers' Guide to Periodical Literature,* for example, lists the periodicals in which up-to-date, brief, and readable information on many subjects can be found. It is an invaluable guide for anyone working on a current events project.

The Readers' Guide to Periodical Literature. New York: The H. W. Wilson Company, 1909–.

Published in pamphlet form once a month during July, August, and February, twice a month the rest of the year. The pamphlets are bound into one-year and two-year volumes. The *Guide* indexes articles printed in about 175 periodicals. Its entries are listed alphabetically according to subject, with subject subdivisions centered under the subject heading. For example:

Guided missiles
Defenses

Under these headings the *Guide* lists, in the following order, the titles of the articles, their authors, the names of the periodicals in which the articles appear, the pages on which the articles may be found, and the date of publication. Frequently the authors' names are missing because many articles in periodicals are unsigned.

Let us suppose you are doing a project on guided missiles. You consult the *Readers' Guide* for the most recent writings on the subject and find the following listing:

Guided missiles
Defenses
Budget choice SALT puts to Pentagon. il
Bus W p 68 Ag 28 '78
Processing of data key to missile defense. il
Aviation W 109:12–15 Ag '78

To understand the abbreviations the *Guide* uses, you will probably need to consult the list of abbreviations given in front of the *Guide*. There you will discover "il" means illustrated, "Bus W" *Business Week,* "Aviation W" *Aviation Week and Space Technology,* "p" page, and "Ag" August.

New York Times Index. New York Times, 1913–.

Published semimonthly, with an annual cumulation, this index gives the exact dates for specific news articles that appeared in *The New York Times* newspaper, along with page numbers and column locations. There are also brief summaries of the major news stories. In many cases these summaries will give you all the information you require, so that you won't have to get hold of the article itself.

ATLASES

An atlas is a collection of maps. A good atlas provides not only detailed maps that show the locations of places but also a vast amount of additional information about those places, such as agriculture, languages spoken, and industries. While much of the same information and even maps may be found in encyclopedias and other reference books, good atlases provide a more extensive collection of maps plus more kinds of maps.

The two most widely known publishers of maps and atlases are Rand McNally and Hammond Incorporated. Both of these companies publish a number of different atlases. The following two are particularly suitable for basic reference work:

Hammond Medallion World Atlas. Maplewood, N.J.: Hammond Incorporated, 1977.

This work contains over 600 maps. All information about a continent, country, state, or province is placed on consecutive pages. The emphasis is on the United States. The contents include historical maps, reproductions of flags, tables of facts about each country, and postal zip code numbers as well.

Rand McNally Cosmopolitan World Atlas. Chicago: Rand McNally and Company, 1978.

The contents of this atlas include oceanographic, political, and metropolitan maps as well as a special twelve-page section of U.S. travel maps. Further, there are numerous tables listing such information as distances between places, principal lakes, rivers, islands, and so on.

GAZETTEERS

A gazetteer is a geographical dictionary. In other words, it lists places alphabetically and usually gives the official spelling of the place, its latitude, longitude, population, and the pronunciation of its name. It also provides historical information about places. In using gazetteers, it is important to note the date of the publication. Names of countries can and do frequently change, along with their boundaries and populations. Nevertheless, gazetteers can be very useful in research. Here are two popular gazetteers:

Columbia Lippincott Gazetteer of the World. New York: Columbia University Press, 1962.

Places of the world are listed in alphabetical order. About 130,000 names with 30,000 cross-references are included.

Webster's New Geographical Dictionary. Springfield, Mass.: G. & C. Merriam, 1977.

This is smaller than the *Columbia Lippincott* but more up to date. It contains 47,000 entries encompassing the usual gazetteer information: location, area, population, altitudes of mountains, length of rivers, and so on.

BIBLIOGRAPHIES

The word *bibliography* means "a list of writings." Annotated bibliographies have descriptive notes with each entry. Suggested reading lists are bibliographies too, and a list of books about a specific subject or by a specific author is also called a bibliography. There are two bound bibliographies that are especially comprehensive. They are, in fact, bibliographies of bibliographies (lists of lists) and are important sources for locating books on any subject at all.

Besterman, Theodore. *A World Bibliography of Bibliographies.* Lausanne: Societas Bibliographica, 1965.

   This book is international in scope. It includes 117,000 items grouped under about 16,000 headings. In 1977 a supplement to this fourth and final edition was published which covers the years 1964 to 1974 (Alice F. Toomey, compiler).

Bibliographic Index. New York: Wilson, 1938–.

   A subject index to bibliographies, which includes listings of English and foreign language reference books, pamphlets, and over 2,400 periodicals.

   Here is a sample from the *Bibliographic Index:*

ALLERGY
Berrens, Lubertus. Chemistry of atopic allergies (Monogs. in allergy, Karger '71 p. 214–290)
Progress in allergy V 23 (25) ed. by Paul Kallos (and others) Karger '77–'78. including bibliography
   See also
      FOOD ALLERGY

BIOGRAPHICAL DICTIONARIES

Biographical dictionaries contain brief sketches of peoples' lives. The people may be real or fictional, American or foreign, living or dead; they may include people of historical importance or people who are in the daily news. These books are among the most-used in the reference library, and libraries carry a wide variety of biographical dictionaries.

The best-known single-volume source of this type is *Webster's Biographical Dictionary.* Also popular, but including only people who are living, is *Who's Who in America.* The multi-volume *Current Biography* offers more substantial information about living people, and the *Dictionary of American Biography* is highly respected for its scholarly approach and objective treatment of its subjects.

Webster's Biographical Dictionary. Springfield, Mass.: G. &. C. Merriam, 1976.

This volume contains 40,000 names of people, living and dead, of all nationalities. The biographies are brief, with just enough facts to identify the person, tell when he or she lived, and mention the person's major accomplishments.

Who's Who in America. Chicago: Marquis, 1899–.

Issued every two years, this is the standard dictionary of contemporary biography. Its 40th edition (1978/79) lists more than 72,000 persons. *Who's Who* aims to include the "best-known men and women in all lines of useful and respectable achievement."

Current Biography. New York: Wilson, 1940–.

Current Biography offers comprehensive accounts of people in the news—important writers, heads of state, industrialists, sports figures, entertainers, and the like. It is published once a month in pamphlet form, then cumulated into annual volumes. Unlike most other reference books of its kind, *Current Biography* includes pictures. To find the biography of a specific person, one has to look through *Current Biography*'s cumulative indexes, published every ten years (1950, 1960, etc.), then in the annual volumes, and finally in the latest monthly issue.

Dictionary of American Biography. New York: Scribner, 1943.

This multi-volume set has long, scholarly articles on over 16,000 noteworthy Americans of the past. It does not include people who are still living. The articles are considered excellent and are signed by the editors or scholars who wrote them.

ALMANACS, YEARBOOKS, AND DIRECTORIES

There are certain books known as "quick" or "ready reference" sources. Yearbooks or other books that serve as concise manuals of specific information and directories that give information about organizations or associations are all designed for quick use. Here are examples of each:

The World Almanac and Book of Facts. New York: Newspaper Enterprise Association, Inc., 1868–.

This book contains up-to-date and reliable information of all kinds, from the amount of gasoline consumed by every make of automobile to the signs of the zodiac. It is replete with statistics and has an alphabetical index of all it contains at the front of the book.

Statesman's Yearbook. New York: St. Martin's Press, 1864–.

This is a concise handbook of information, mainly in statistical form, about governments of the world. It is published annually.

Here is a sample of some material published in the book:

(under GUAM)
TRADE. Guam is the only American territory which is completely "free trade"; excise duties are levied only upon imports of tobacco, liquid fuel, and liquor. In the year ending 30 June 1976 imports were valued at $266.3 m. and accounted for 91% of trade.

Encyclopedia of Associations. Detroit: Gale Research, 1956–.

Organized in three volumes and brought up to date yearly since 1975 (biannually before that), this directory lists all kinds of organizations, including business, legal, military, cultural, veterans, sports, and labor organizations just to name a few.

Here is a sample of the book's entries:

PEOPLE-TO-PEOPLE INTERNATIONAL
(International Relations)
2440 Pershing Rd., G-30
Kansas City, MO 64108
Phone: (816) 421–6343
James T. Doty, Pres.
Founded: 1956. **Staff:** 6. Organization of private citizens who communicate voluntarily with people of other countries through letters, campus and classroom projects, travel abroad. . . .

AUDIO-VISUAL SOURCES

Libraries have many kinds of audio-visual materials: pictures (including postcards), slides, filmstrips, films, phonograph records, tapes, and microforms. These materials are especially helpful for studying music, art, history, and literature. Seeing the reproduction of a work of art like the Mona Lisa or listening to the tape of a President speak may make your understanding of an artist or of a period in American history that much more clear. These audio-visual materials may or may not be listed in your library's card catalog, so a familiarity with the guides and indexes to them is especially important. Here are a few of those guides:

Educational Media Index. Educational Media Council. New York: McGraw-Hill, 1964.

This is a 14-volume guide to the sources, contents, and costs of films, kinescopes, filmstrips, slides, pictures, videotapes, and more.

Educator's Guide. Randolph, Wis.: Educators Progress Service.

This service publishes the *Educator's Guide to Free Films* (1941–), the *Educator's Guide to Free Filmstrips* (1949–), and the *Educator's Guide to Free Audio and Video Materials* (1955–). These annual guides contain lists of all the available materials arranged by subject, with a subject and title index.

Guide to Educational Media: Films, Filmstrips, Kinescopes, Phonodiscs, Phonotapes, Programmed Instruction Materials, Slides, Transparencies, Videotapes. Rusvold, Margaret I. and Guss, Carolyn. Chicago: American Library Association, 1971.

This is a guide to catalogs, periodicals, and organizations that give information on nonbook materials.

MICROFORMS

The word microform is used to describe various kinds of materials that are microprinted—photographically reduced in size—such as microfilm, microprint, and microfiche (a sheet of microfilm). Photographing the pages of newspapers, magazines, documents, and other printed materials in this manner obviously permits the storing of huge quantities of reading matter in a comparatively small space. Many libraries today house a variety of microform materials and, of course, the reading machines that illuminate and enlarge the print on the microforms, so that the contents may be easily and comfortably read.

Usually, a library includes a listing of its microform collection in its card catalog. Sometimes the collection is listed separately and kept at the library's reference desk. If you don't know where the listing is in your library, ask the librarian. Don't ignore these valuable resources. It is well worth the effort to locate them.

After a while, as you become more experienced in the use of all the reference material the library has to offer, you will know without thinking which encyclopedia, atlas, index, etc., to go to in order to find quickly the information you want. This should make your research task not only less tedious but more productive as well.

Specialized
Reference Sources

There are times when a general reference work will not give you as much information or the kind of information you need. For example you may be doing a report on the history of baseball, a paper on the story of jazz, an analysis of a specific period in the history of art, or an explanation of some very technical scientific principle. For information in these areas you might do better to consult one of the library's more specialized reference books. Just as there are *general* encyclopedias, indexes, dictionaries, and so on, so there are *specialized* encyclopedias, indexes, dictionaries, and the like, and their authors, titles, and subject matter are all listed in the library's card catalog.

A word of caution. These specialized reference books are not to be considered as useful to basic research as are the general reference books. The data in the specialized books becomes outdated fairly quickly. Rules in the sports world change from time to time, viewpoints in the art world shift quite frequently, scientific theories can change almost daily, and so on. Always note the date of publication in any specialized reference book you use. It will help you to better evaluate the accuracy of the book's information.

There are several hundred such specialized research books in the library, covering a number of categories. We will review some of the available sources in just two of these categories. It is fair to assume that their equivalents exist to a fair degree in other categories such as theater, education, photography, music, archeology, and sports.

ART

Encyclopedia of World Art. New York: McGraw-Hill Book Company, Inc., 1959–1968. 15 volumes.

This book contains biographies of artists, different periods in the history of art, art concepts, and problems of art.

Larousse Encyclopedia of Modern Art, from 1800 to the Present Day. Huyghe, René, ed. New York: Prometheus Press, 1965.

One of a series of such books, translated from the French, showing the art of the period in relation to the philosophy, literature, science, and social and economic conditions of the time.

McGraw-Hill Dictionary of Art. New York: McGraw-Hill, 1969. 5 volumes.

This dictionary contains long articles on the lives and careers of the artists listed, artistic styles, art periods, art buildings and museums, and art terms.

Art Index. January 1929–. New York: Wilson, 1930–.

This is a quarterly index of authors and subject matter appearing in about 205 American and foreign periodicals.

American Art Directory. New York: Bowker, 1899–.

This is a directory of museums, art organizations, university art departments, and art schools and classes in the United States, Canada, and abroad.

Art Prices Current. London: Art Trade Press, 1908–.

This publication lists the sale prices (of art) at the principal London, Continental, and American auction rooms, arranged in chronological order, by sales.

Art Through the Ages. Gardner, Helen. New York: Harcourt, 1975. 6th edition.

This is a standard work that is used widely as a basic textbook in high schools, colleges, and universities.

Guide to Art Reference Books. Chamberlin, Mary Walls. Chicago: American Library Association, 1959.

This guide lists more than 2,500 titles, ranging from ready reference to highly specialized works.

Art Reproductions. Clapp, Jane. New York: Scarecrow, 1961.

This book lists the art reproductions available in ninety-five museums in the United States and Canada.

Handbook of Legendary and Mythological Art. Boston: Houghton, 1892.

This volume deals with symbolism in art, with legends and stories illustrated in art.

SCIENCE

McGraw-Hill Encyclopedia of Science and Technology. New York: McGraw-Hill, 1971. 4th edition.

This is a comprehensive encyclopedia that covers all branches of science and technology. It is kept up to date with the publication of yearbooks.

Applied Science and Technology Index. New York: Wilson, 1913–.

This publication, published monthly (except July), with quarterly and annual cumulations, contains a subject index to about 280 English language science periodicals.

Dictionary of Science and Technology. Collocott, T. C., ed. London: Chambers, 1971, New York: Barnes & Noble, 1972.

This book provides an alphabetical listing of scientific and technological terms, with short definitions of each.

World Who's Who in Science. Debus, Allen G., ed. Chicago: Marquis, 1968.

This is a biographical dictionary of notable scientists from antiquity to the present. It contains about 30,000 entries. It is international in its coverage but is most complete in its coverage of American scientists.

Scientific, Technical and Related Societies of the United States. Washington, D.C.: National Academy of Sciences, 1971–.

Information in this publication includes the officers of the different societies, background and history of the societies, their purpose and scope of activities, membership, services, meetings, activities, and publications.

Britannica Yearbook of Science and the Future. Chicago: Encyclopedia Britannica, 1968–.

This yearbook (none listed in the 1979 *Books in Print*) offers up-to-date information on scientific and technological subjects and is geared to readers with little background in science.

As with everything else in the library, if you have difficulty finding the specialized reference book you want, you may be certain that the librarian will be glad to help you.

Part Three

Locating Sources
for a Project

Before you begin research in the library, it is best to know exactly what you are looking for. Do you want general information, perhaps the largest rivers in the world or the different kinds of animals that are found in Africa? Or is it the life of an author, a scientist, or a President you seek? Are you looking for statistics such as the number of people who live in each state of the United States, the batting average of Joe DiMaggio in 1950, or the percentage of undernourished children in different countries? If you figure out in advance precisely the kind of information you need for your report or speech, you will save yourself considerable time in research.

Sometimes the best approach is to start with an encyclopedia. The encyclopedia might be a general one, like the *Americana* or the *Britannica;* or, if you are researching in a particular subject, such as art or medicine, then you would use an art or a medical encyclopedia. An encyclopedia will give you statistics, background, and a survey of the subject. Sometimes this kind of research will be enough for your purposes. If not, then you will have to move to the card catalog to help locate the additional information you need.

We've already described the catalog and told you how to use it. Here are some additional pointers that will help you find the information you want more easily.

You know that when the first word in the title of a book is "A" or "An" or "The," it will be omitted from the catalog card. *A History of Latin America* will appear as *History of Latin America* in the catalog. You look for that card under "H," not "A." Similarly, *The Kingdom and the Power* will appear as *Kingdom and the Power,* under "K," not "T."

If the author's name is M'Carthy, McCarthy, or MacCarthy, you will find it in the catalog as if it were spelled MacCarthy. You may not run across this problem often, but it is good to be prepared for it.

Sometimes there is no individual author of a book. In fact, a good number of books are published by organizations, with the organization listed as author of the volume. Government agencies, such as health departments, agricultural departments, and departments of state, issue leaflets and books. There are organizations such as the National Audubon Society and UNICEF that publish pamphlets and books. You will find such reading materials listed in the catalog with the organization or association as author.

If you are looking for a book whose title begins with a number, you will find that number spelled out: *One Hundred Days of Solitude, Seventeen, Forty Days at Musa Dagh, Fifty Great Mystery Stories,* and so on.

You will also usually find abbreviations in the title of a book spelled out. It will be *Doctor Zhivago,* not *Dr. Zhivago.* It will be *Captain Cook,* not *Capt. Cook.* However, this rule in cataloging is not universal. Some libraries do use abbreviations in their catalog cards for such titles.

Now let us suppose that you have no names of books or authors for the subject of your report. How do you approach the cards in the library catalog? It seems that you have a most difficult task to perform. Actually, it is not difficult at all. All you need to do is to locate the subject matter on a card in the catalog.

For example, if you are writing a report on nutrition, you will surely find a card in the catalog marked *Nutrition.* In fact, you are very likely to find a number of cards marked *Nutrition.* Some will list books that deal with the science of nutrition, others that deal with nutrition and health, and perhaps there will be a few concerned with nutrition in various parts of the world. You will also, most likely, be referred by one or another of the cards to the topic, say, *Vitamins.* And that will lead you to more listings of books you may want for your report.

If you are going to write a report on baseball, and you are not quite certain about the precise nature of the report you want to turn in, you might look among the catalog cards under *World Series, National League, Minor Leagues,* or even *Japan.* The cards will lead you to books that will help you decide on an exact topic for your report.

If you have any difficulty finding cards under the title you have in mind, you might look through the catalog cards for a title that is similar.

As already indicated, if you cannot find *Nutrition,* you most likely will find *Vitamins,* or vice versa. If you are doing a book on housing and cannot find a card marked *Housing,* try finding a card marked *Urban Development.* If there is no card labeled *Baseball,* look for a card labeled *Sports.*

Remember, too, that the librarian is always there to help you find the books you need for your report.

Using
Reference Books

There are several simple but very important rules to follow when using the books you have selected for your reference materials. Follow these rules and you will save much time and effort.

First, as soon as you locate information you think you will use in your report, write down the name of the book in which you found the information. Write down the name of the author. If you find the information in a magazine, write down the date of the magazine, along with the title of the article and its author. Write down the page or pages on which you have located the information you are going to use.

You follow this procedure for two reasons. One, you will be able to locate the material again, in case you want to check on a word, a sentence, or perhaps some statistics. Secondly, you can always refer to the precise location of your information, in case you are questioned by either your teacher or classmates for the source of your material.

Once you have the reference book you want for your report, examine its table of contents. You won't need the entire book for your report, and the table of contents will direct you to the one or two chapters in the book that deal with the topic of your report. If the book has an index, you should look at that too. The index, very likely, will send you to pages of needed information that you might miss otherwise.

For example, if you are doing a report on China, the index of the book might include "France," "Great Britain," "piracy," "resistance," and "revolts," among other listings, and all these subjects might appear in different parts of the book. If you are doing a report on genealogy, the index of the book may list "anglicizing of," "errors in," "family nomenclature," and "spelling of," all subjects that might prove useful to you, yet appear in different parts of the book.

Sometimes in the back of the book you may find appendixes that prove helpful to your report. You are sure to find many appendixes in sports books, since these books are always full of important statistics. A book on conservation might well have an appendix on major accomplishments in the area of saving forests or cleaning up rivers. A book on the history of the United States might have a chronology of important dates in the appendix plus a listing of the Amendments to the Constitution and the Presidents of the United States. Appendixes are often stocked with excellent material for research reports.

Some books have a glossary at the end. A glossary contains, in alphabetical order, explanations of certain words, for example, scientific words or foreign language words. Sometimes a glossary will contain short biographies of people discussed in the book. Glossaries will help you better understand the material you are reading, as well as supply you with considerable new information.

Finally, there are sometimes footnotes to the main text of the book. A footnote is usually an added thought, perhaps a comment on a statement of fact in the book or an opinion. It may provide additional information, statistics, or even an opinion opposing the original opinion cited. It may provide the source for a fact or an opinion—the name, date, title of book or periodical, etc. Sometimes it will offer an explanation of some fact, comment, or opinion in the book.

It would be wise for the researcher to read these notes. In addition to providing more material for a report, these notes may very well lead to further valuable sources.

Of course, you should be sure to check the date of publication of the book you are using. This has been said before, but it bears repeating. The more up-to-date the publication, the more accurate the contents of the book are likely to be. A book printed many years ago may contain information no longer true. For example, if you are doing a report on West Africa, an old book will have a section on the Gold Coast. But the Gold Coast no longer exists. In 1957 the Gold Coast became Ghana. Ghana, incidentally, in a book that was printed many years ago, would refer to an ancient empire that has not existed for more than a thousand years.

Judging
Research Material

When you examine batting averages, football statistics, dates of discoveries, the size of different countries or states of the United States, you are fairly certain that what you are reading is accurate. There are some facts, however, in the books you examine, that should be questioned. The old saying is, "Don't believe everything you read," and there is much wisdom in that old saw. It doesn't mean that you must doubt everything you read; it suggests, rather, that you examine what you read for possible error or personal bias, as well as for errors due to faulty scholarship.

Let us examine these possible errors, what may cause them, and how to judge research material accordingly.

If you read of the American Revolution in a book written by an Englishman, more often than not, the revolution will be treated simply as a mistake in Britain's dealing with its American colonies.

A book on the Civil War written by a Northerner may be quite different from a similar book written by a Southerner. The Northern writer may give credit to General Robert E. Lee; the Southern writer may glorify him. General Ulysses S. Grant may be a hero to the Northern writer. He is often something less than a hero to the Southern writer.

A Russian writing on the Soviet Union will almost surely turn out a book quite different from a book an American would turn out on the Soviet Union. One can assume that a labor leader's statement on working conditions will be quite different from a statement of those conditions by the owners of the factory, mill, or mine operation. A woman's viewpoint on discrimination against women will be different, most likely, from the viewpoint of a man.

What we are talking about is *bias.* The bias may come about because of different interpretations of the same fact. A student may say that he or she is getting too much homework; a teacher may say that the homework load is required for good learning and is not too heavy. The worker may say that he or she is not paid enough for the work; the employer may say that the worker is being paid the same as everyone else doing the kind of job that is being performed. In each of these cases, both parties may be making "correct" statements. It is your job as a researcher to be aware of who it is that is making the statement and to judge the statement in as unbiased a manner as possible.

Notice the phrase "as possible." We all have biases. If you come from a family of workers, you will tend to give a worker's point of view great weight; if your parents own a shop, you are likely to believe a statement made by the owner of a shop. This is quite normal. However, again, as a researcher you must rid yourself of your biases as much as possible.

There are other ways of judging the accuracy of what you read. For example, how qualified is the author of the book you are reading? In other words, what are his or her credentials?

If it is a science book you are reading, say a book on nuclear energy, what is the experience of the author with nuclear energy? Is he or she a respected scientist? A teacher of science? How much has he or she written on energy? What is the reaction of other scientists to the theories being discussed?

Immanuel Velikovsky has written a number of books in the area of science, and each of those books has met with severe criticism from the scientific world. Velikovsky has come up with a number of theories that have been completely rejected, even laughed at, by scientists. If you read Velikovsky, do you reject him completely too, laugh at him, or do you try to make your own judgment of his work? Only you can answer this.

If the book you are reading is about another state, a foreign country, or a people with whom you are not familiar—say, the Maori of New Zealand or the nomads of central Asia—you would want to know two things. First, has the writer visited these countries and these people, and if so, for how long? Second, how does the writer feel about these countries and their people; is he or she sympathetic and understanding? Does the author accept the people for who they are, or does he or she expect them to live and behave like Americans?

Some people spend no more than a few days, or a few weeks at most, in a country, then write a huge book on their experiences. Some people expect every country to have refrigerators, microwave ovens, and taxis. Some people are even irritated because everyone doesn't speak English. Keep these things in mind when you judge the value of a book on other people and other places.

Judging research materials may not be a simple task, but it is *essential* for accurate reporting.

You and the Librarian

You have been told several times now that the librarian is always ready and willing to help you find the research material you need for your project. This is particularly true when you approach the librarian with patience and with well thought out, intelligent questions.

Often there is only one librarian in a library, who sits at a desk conveniently located in the room. He or she is the prime source for basic information about the library and its collection. Sometimes there are several people around that desk waiting to speak to the librarian. Or, the librarian may be away from the desk helping another person locate material. Do not be impatient. Wait your turn, or wait patiently for the librarian to return. Good research can be time-consuming, but it is time well spent.

Try to make the questions you ask precise. Come to the library prepared with your question or questions:

"I'm giving a talk on famous speeches by great Americans. It's for my ninth-grade English class. Can you help me?"

You have given the librarian all the information he or she needs to help you: the precise subject matter and the level at which you intend to report. The librarian will take it from there.

Most times you will know the precise area in which you wish to do your research. Most often, too, it will be a limited area, a clearly defined area, one that you can deal with without too much difficulty. In such cases, an encyclopedia and one or two books on the subject will provide all the material you need.

Let us say, however, that your report is on a controversial issue—for example, the drug leatrile. In such cases, you will want to find material on both sides of the issue, perhaps include statements made by those who are for the drug and those who are against it. You are not likely to find one book that presents both sides of the argument. Nor are you likely to find an entry on leatrile in an encyclopedia. You will need a lot of help from your librarian.

Most likely, you will be directed to the *Readers' Guide*. The *Readers' Guide,* you will recall, lists all articles written on all subjects and the periodicals in which these articles can be found. More than likely too, if the librarian is not too busy, he or she will help you locate in the *Readers' Guide* the articles you need and perhaps even the articles themselves.

Finally, there are times when you are not really certain what the precise subject matter of your report should be. You know that you want to report on something in aeronautics, but aeronautics is a huge subject. Again, the librarian can help, if you state exactly what is troubling you:

"I want to do a report on aeronautics for my science class, but I don't know whether to report on early experiments in aviation, on myths about aviation, on the supersonic transport jet, or what. Can you help me?"

Research Notes

Research will usually require the writing of notes—phrases, whole sentences, whole paragraphs, sometimes even dates or numbers. Prepare yourself for the occasion with enough paper and perhaps several pens or sharpened pencils.

You can take notes as you read, then organize them when you get home, but a better idea would be to organize *before* you go to the library, perhaps by heading separate sheets of paper with different topics. For example, if your report is on the life of T. S. Eliot, you might have one blank sheet headed *Childhood,* another *Boyhood,* a third *Jobs,* a fourth *Important Writings,* a fifth *Honors Won,* and so on. Then, as you gather material, you will have a special slot waiting for each bit of information you find. When you get home, you will have a much easier time collating all the material you found in the library.

Again, when you copy something you wish to quote in a report or speech, be certain you have copied every word and every punctuation mark exactly as you found it in your source material, and be sure to note down all the important information concerning the source—author, date, etc.

When you list statistics, it is generally a good idea to check them perhaps more than once against the source from which you are taking them. Precision and exactness are essential to good research work.

Index

Research notes, 56–57
Roots, 3

Science, 39–41
Scientific, Technical and Related Societies of the United States, 40
See also cross-reference cards, 14, 16
See cross-reference cards, 14, 15
Statesman's Yearbook, 34
Statistics, 33, 34, 49, 57
Subject cards, 47
Subject catalog, 17

Table of contents, 48
Title catalog, 17

Unabridged dictionaries, 26–27

Velikovsky, Immanuel, 53

Webster's Biographical Dictionary, 32
Webster's New Geographical Dictionary, 30
Webster's Third New International Dictionary of the English Language, 26–27
Who's Who in America, 32
World Almanac and Book of Facts, 33
World Bibliography of Bibliographies, 31
World Who's Who in Science, 40

Yearbooks, 33, 34

Zip code numbers, 29

About the Author

Bernice MacDonald is currently a librarian and Associate Director of the Branch Libraries of The New York Public Library. *How to Use Reference Materials* is her first book for Franklin Watts. Ms. MacDonald was born in New York State and has worked in many New York City neighborhood libraries.